The
Voyager's Stone

A Richard Jackson Book

The Voyager's Stone

The Adventures of a
Message-Carrying Bottle
Adrift on the Ocean Sea

by ROBERT KRASKE

illustrated by BRIAN FLOCA

ORCHARD BOOKS · New York

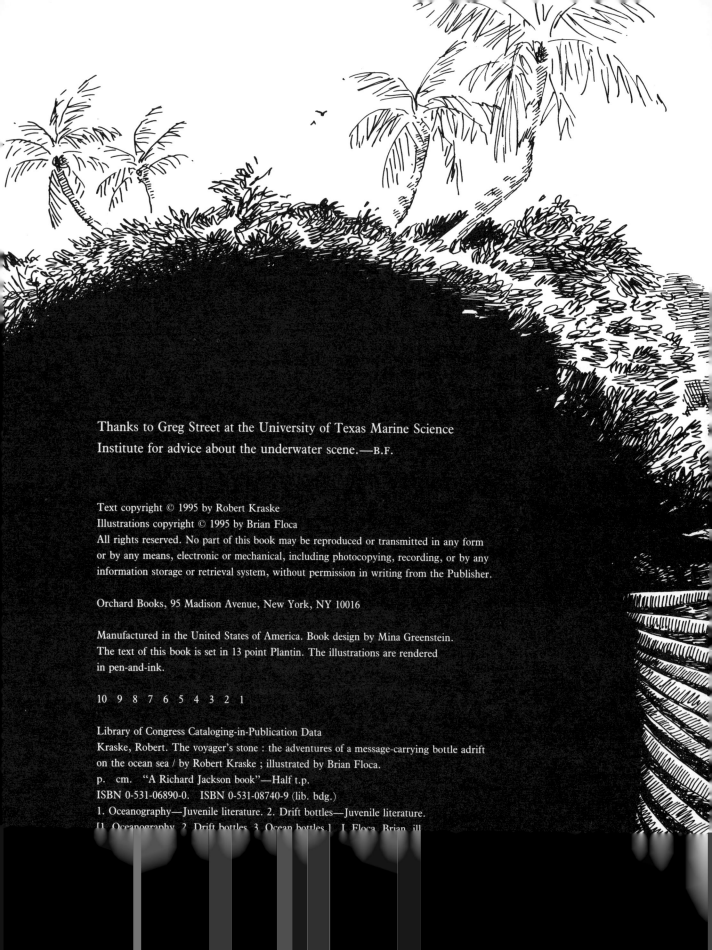

Thanks to Greg Street at the University of Texas Marine Science
Institute for advice about the underwater scene.—B.F.

Orchard Books, 95 Madison Avenue, New York, NY 10016

Manufactured in the United States of America. Book design by Mina Greenstein.
The text of this book is set in 13 point Plantin. The illustrations are rendered
in pen-and-ink.

10 9 8 7 6 5 4 3 2 1

Library of Congress Cataloging-in-Publication Data
Kraske, Robert. The voyager's stone : the adventures of a message-carrying bottle adrift
on the ocean sea / by Robert Kraske ; illustrated by Brian Floca.
p.   cm.   "A Richard Jackson book"—Half t.p.
ISBN 0-531-06890-0.   ISBN 0-531-08740-9 (lib. bdg.)
1. Oceanography—Juvenile literature. 2. Drift bottles—Juvenile literature.
[1. Oceanography. 2. Drift bottles. 3. Ocean bottles.] I. Floca, Brian, ill.

For Ésther, Erik, and Kady
—R.K.

For Todd, Rob, Tim, and Samantha
—B.F.

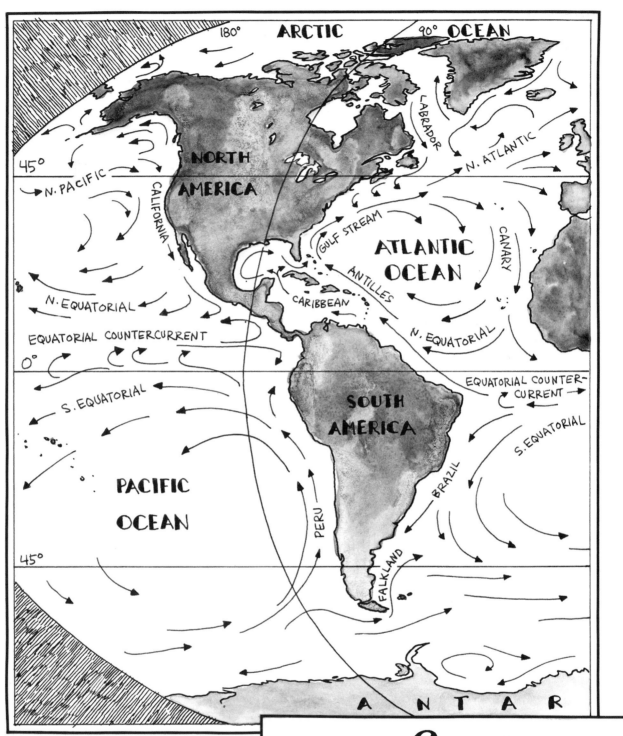

ARCTIC 90° OCEAN

180°

45°

NORTH
AMERICA

N. PACIFIC

CALIFORNIA

LABRADOR

N. ATLANTIC

GULF STREAM

ATLANTIC
OCEAN

CANARY

ANTILLES

N. EQUATORIAL

CARIBBEAN

N. EQUATORIAL

EQUATORIAL COUNTERCURRENT

0°

S. EQUATORIAL

EQUATORIAL COUNTER-
CURRENT

SOUTH
AMERICA

S. EQUATORIAL

PACIFIC

OCEAN

BRAZIL

PERU

45°

FALKLAND

A N T A R

The Setting of

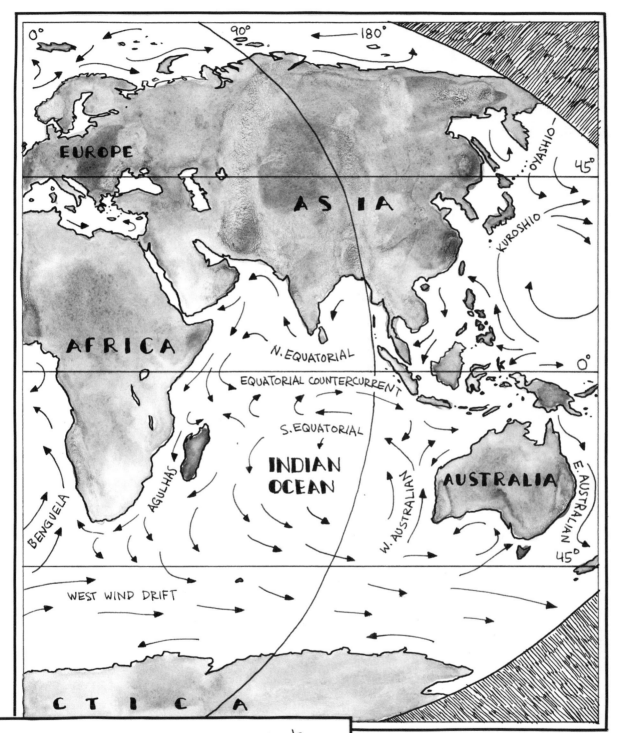

the Voyage

A BOY SAT ON A FLAT ROCK NEAR THE EDGE OF A CLIFF HIGH ABOVE THE SEA.

Between his knees he held a bottle. Carefully he rolled a message and a snapshot of himself and poked them through the bottle's neck. Then he dropped in a tiny polished stone—a Voyager's Stone, a special charm. He twisted a cork into the bottle and tapped it tight.

In his school library, the boy had read a book about messages found in seagoing bottles. Some had drifted for years, nearly around the world, before floating ashore.

He held the clear glass bottle to his chest and looked out across the water. Where would his adventurer end up? On the sandy beach of a distant island? In a seaport busy with passenger liners and cargo ships? In the stomach of a whale?

He wished he could shrink in size—close up small like a telescope— like Alice in Wonderland—climb inside the bottle and go exploring. . . .

Below, the long waves of the Caribbean Sea rolled toward the island. Pushed by the steady trade wind from the Atlantic Ocean, the swells dashed against the cliff face, flinging sheets of salt spray high into the sunlit air.

The smooth rock the boy sat on was called Hood's Seat. He had read, in a booklet given to all visitors to the island, that the notorious pirate Captain Hood had once sat on this very rock training his spyglass to the northeast. Each day he had watched for English warships sent to capture him.

A sundial carved in a stone post stood nearby. A shadow cast by the sun on the dial showed the time—nearly eleven o'clock.

"Colton! Where are you?"

Startled, the boy looked over his shoulder down the shaded path between palm trees.

"Colt? I told you to stay out of the sun!"

He stood on the rock. His right arm drew back to throw the bottle. But it was too round and smooth. He couldn't grip it firmly.

"Colton!"

He grasped the bottle by its neck, set to try an underarm throw, like tossing a ball to a batter. With a little jump as his arm swung forward, he flung the bottle past the cliff edge.

"I christen thee . . . Voyager!" he cried.

But the bottle, instead of curving far out over the sea, flew nearly straight up, turning end over end, then plummeted past the cliff, barely missing the edge.

Alarmed, the boy tried to look over the cliff, but was afraid to get too close to the edge. The bottle—Voyager—was surely lost, smashed against the cliff face by an incoming wave.

"Colton! Colton! Are you up there?"

HIGH ABOVE THE BLUE WATER, a frigate bird soared on seven-foot wings. Its dark eyes scanned the sea below, searching for dinner—small fish, a newborn squid, a drifting jellyfish. A masterful flier, the bird glided skyward in slow circles.

Far below there was movement. A small dolphin chased a flying fish. The three-foot-long hunter body-surfed down a wave and burst from the water in a long leap as it pursued the airborne fish.

The frigate bird half folded its long wings, closed its forked tail, and hurtled down. Barely a foot above the waves, it swooped out of its dive and hovered, its wings fanning the air. When the flying fish emerged again, the frigate was waiting. It nabbed the unlucky flier in its long beak and quickly swallowed. Turning into the wind, it sailed upward.

The weather in the Caribbean in mid-December was at its finest. Fluffy clouds sailed in a blue sky.

Now the frigate hung nearly motionless in the light air, its eyes fixed on an island below. Waves climbed thirty feet up a hundred-foot cliff, only to drop back and mount a new charge.

From its high position, the bird caught a glint of light as an object flew out from the cliff and into the clear air. Tumbling end over end, the object struck the back of a wave as it slid away from the rock.

The frigate dived. Near the surface, it braked and hovered.

What the bird saw was a clear glass bottle bobbing in the water. A human eye as close as the frigate's would have made out a message inside. A tiny stone clinked against the glass as the bottle lifted and fell in the low waves.

The bird needed only a moment to determine that the object could not be eaten. Extending its wings, it soared aloft and resumed scanning the sea.

A flock of gulls hovered over a school of tiny yellow fish rising to the surface. Their excited cries carried far in the sunlit air. The frigate bird leaned in that direction and glided down.

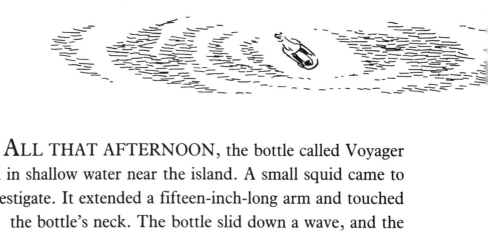

ALL THAT AFTERNOON, the bottle called Voyager drifted in shallow water near the island. A small squid came to investigate. It extended a fifteen-inch-long arm and touched the bottle's neck. The bottle slid down a wave, and the startled squid jetted away, its arms trailing behind.

The water was clear eighteen feet down. On the bottom, a three-hundred-pound green turtle fed on ribbonlike seaweed. Snails the size of baseballs crept over the sand among horny green-conch shells.

A flying fish shot out of the waves and curved into the wind. To become airborne, the fish sprinted through the water, its tail beating fifty times per second. Lifting from the water, it opened long fins and glided at thirty-five miles per hour for a hundred and fifty feet before entering the water again.

Finger-long fish swam by the bottle, the sun striking their silvery flanks, then darted away as a hunter-fish gave chase. Gulls appeared, hovering and crying, waiting for the tiny fish to resurface.

A brief rain shower pattered the sea in the afternoon, and then sunshine returned.

In the evening, as the sun sank among streaks of orange, yellow, and violet clouds, the bottle bobbed in a small cove bordered with palm trees.

A "sea bean"—a coconut—floated in the low surf a few yards away. The green nut had drifted north for four months after dropping from a tree at the mouth of the Amazon River in Brazil.

A wave sent the drifter rolling onto the beach. Succeeding waves and a steady wind would carry the nut up the sand. Days of rain and hot sun would cause the green color to fade to brown. In a few months, the dark brown husk would send up a leafy shoot. In time, roots would break through the shell, and a new palm tree would begin to grow.

The moon was full that night—yellow and pink—as the bottle lingered in the shallows. The wind blew across the island at a steady twenty miles per hour, rustling the palm leaves. Among the trees, bats flew zigzag patterns to feed on insects.

In the morning, rose-colored clouds massed on the horizon. The outgoing tide carried the bottle out of the shallows. It floated among strands of yellow seaweed. Before the bottle called Voyager lay the shining ocean sea.

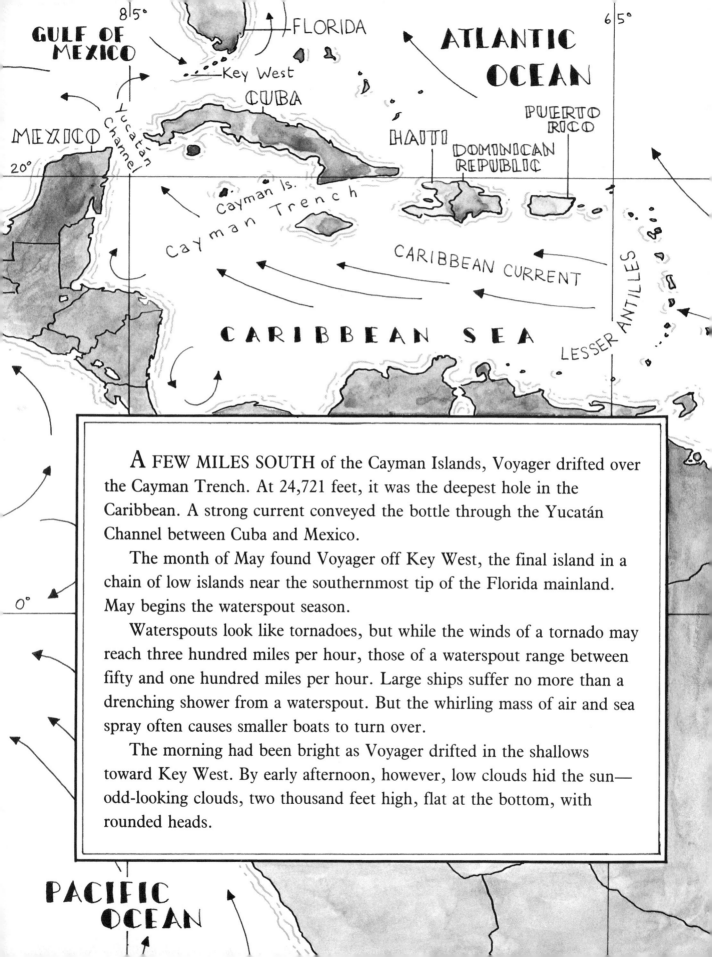

GULF OF
MEXICO

Key West

ATLANTIC
OCEAN

CUBA

PUERTO
RICO

MEXICO

HAITI

DOMINICAN
REPUBLIC

20°

Cayman Is.

Cayman Trench

CARIBBEAN CURRENT

CARIBBEAN SEA

LESSER ANTILLES

0°

A FEW MILES SOUTH of the Cayman Islands, Voyager drifted over the Cayman Trench. At 24,721 feet, it was the deepest hole in the Caribbean. A strong current conveyed the bottle through the Yucatán Channel between Cuba and Mexico.

The month of May found Voyager off Key West, the final island in a chain of low islands near the southernmost tip of the Florida mainland. May begins the waterspout season.

Waterspouts look like tornadoes, but while the winds of a tornado may reach three hundred miles per hour, those of a waterspout range between fifty and one hundred miles per hour. Large ships suffer no more than a drenching shower from a waterspout. But the whirling mass of air and sea spray often causes smaller boats to turn over.

The morning had been bright as Voyager drifted in the shallows toward Key West. By early afternoon, however, low clouds hid the sun—odd-looking clouds, two thousand feet high, flat at the bottom, with rounded heads.

PACIFIC
OCEAN

One cloud poked down, shaped like a funnel. It churned the water, sucking up sea spray. The funnel turned faster and faster. It roared like an express train in a tunnel.

Eighty feet wide at the cloud and forty feet wide at the water, the roaring column of air and spray advanced across a spit of sand. The whirling funnel bent coconut trees and sucked up sand, leaves, branches, worms, frogs, and rats that could not crawl, swim, jump, or run from its path.

In the shallows, Voyager was caught in the churning water and lifted high into the funnel—higher and higher. As the bottle reached the cloud base some twenty-two hundred feet above the sea, the waterspout suddenly collapsed. In a shower of rain, Voyager dropped, tumbling end over end, the stone rattling against the glass. Its speed increased to 256 miles per hour. After a free fall of twelve seconds, it struck the sea, cork and neck down.

Down through the water it sped, streaming bubbles from its sides. Twenty-five feet below the surface, it lodged in soft sand. Its neck jammed under a waterlogged coconut-tree trunk. The tree had been uprooted from its island home in a hurricane years earlier and blown into the sea. Under the old trunk, Voyager was firmly wedged.

THE UNDERWATER WORLD was quiet and peaceful. Yellow
shafts of sunlight filtered through the clear green water. Silver bubbles
trickled up to the surface.

Around the bottle was an underwater garden. Colorful fish—spotted,
striped, speckled, yellow, black, blue-neon—grazed among the grass.
Oysters, barnacles, and sponges littered the white sand. Prickly sea
urchins prowled the bottom. A red-banded shrimp lifted tiny pincers. A
spidery starfish crawled over a sponge. Dense patches of turtle grass
provided homes for small fish. A balloonfish lingered near the bottom,
ready to puff itself up into too large a meal for the mouths of hunter-fish.
A school of slender barracuda sped by, their long jaws revealing sharp
triangular teeth.

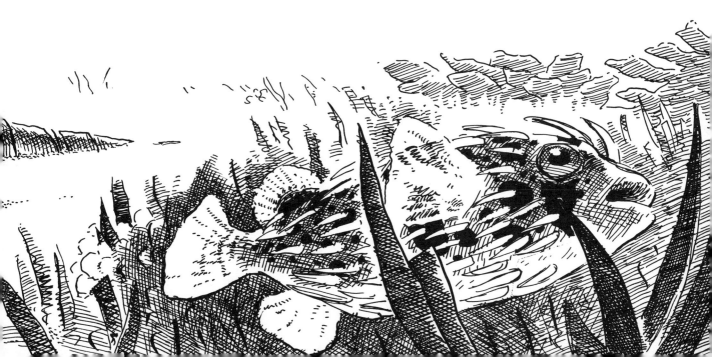

Into this scene appeared an octopus. It "walked" by reaching out an arm, gripping a rock with suction disks, then pulling itself along. A large octopus, it was fourteen feet across, arm tip to arm tip. Its boneless body flowed gracefully across the sea floor, like a scarf in a breeze.

The octopus drew itself to the sunken tree trunk, then froze when it spotted the strange object. An arm moved out, slid down the length of the bottle, and withdrew. Somewhere in its brain, the sea creature recognized the object as not eatable.

At that moment, a lobster emerged from behind a rock, swimming backward. Instantly the octopus snaked out an arm. While that arm held the struggling lobster, the tip of another arm probed the joints of the legs, picking out the meat without damaging the outer shell. Pieces of the lobster passed from disk to disk, from the tip of the arm to the mouth.

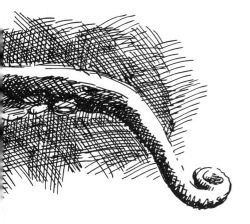

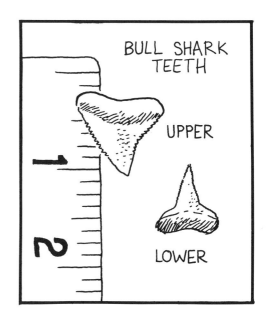

BULL SHARK
TEETH

UPPER

LOWER

The struggles of the lobster attracted a shark. Out of the blue depths it came, weaving from side to side, its long snout sensing prey, showing a row of teeth in its underslung jaw, edges jagged like a steak knife, good for sawing and tearing flesh and muscle.

The shark was almost twelve feet long, blue on its back, white on its underside. It circled, its black, unblinking eyes watching the octopus. Unlike most fish, the shark had no bladder filled with air to keep it afloat. It had to keep moving or it would sink. Constant movement also helped to keep water flowing across its gills to transfer oxygen in the water to its bloodstream and enable it to "breathe."

The octopus, its color changing to dark red and then to gray, dropped the lobster. It rose stiffly to its full height on long arms. Its eyes bulged from its head like doorknobs as it carefully followed the moves of its enemy.

The shark would have preferred a smaller victim, but it was hungry and the large octopus was there. It darted back and forth, back and forth, all the while drawing nearer and nearer to its prey.

On one close sweep, it suddenly whipped around and dived, its jaws open, but the octopus dodged sideways.

The shark whirled, and dived again, and the octopus slid backward, watching every move of its deadly foe.

Another lunge by the shark. But this time, instead of dodging, the octopus sidestepped. As the shark passed, the octopus snaked an arm around its victim. The speed of the shark tore the octopus off the bottom. Instantly it wrapped all eight arms around the shark.

Now the shark became frantic. Eyes rolling upward, it dashed to and fro. It sped to the surface, leaped into the air, and fell back in a mighty splash upon the octopus. Still the octopus clung like a rider on a bucking horse. Slowly two arms slid forward over the shark's gills.

The shark slackened its rush, spurted suddenly, then spun around like a pinwheel. But now it was weakening. It sank to the bottom. A few final twitches of its tail, then a shudder passed along its sleek body, and it lay still.

The octopus held the gills of the shark closed until the killer died. Then, arms still wrapped about the shark, the octopus floated away on the light current, carrying its attacker.

For two nights, the bottle lay in the black water under the tree trunk. In the late afternoon of the third day, as the water was again darkening, a green turtle appeared. Ignoring the bottle, it fed on the long grass along the bottom. As it moved to a new clump of grass, a single swipe of its powerful front flipper dislodged the bottle from under the sunken tree trunk.

Air trapped inside lifted Voyager, and it broke through the surface of the water. The sun was sinking on the western horizon. Voyager floated in splashes of reds and golds until the water turned black and night came.

8 5°

7 5°

GULF OF
MEXICO

GULF STREAM

FLORIDA

Miami

ATLANTIC
OCEAN

25°

15°

CARIBBEAN CURRENT

A LONG THE EAST COAST OF FLORIDA, NEAR MIAMI, THE GULF STREAM FLOWS AT FOUR TO FIVE MILES

per hour. "A river in the ocean," oceanographers call it. Fifty miles wide and fifteen hundred feet deep, the Gulf Stream's current is so strong that large ships use it to travel north, saving time and fuel. Their speed increases from a normal 16.5 knots to up to 20.5 knots—from 19 to nearly 24 miles per hour.

Drifting in the Gulf Stream near Florida, Voyager was overtaken by a Portuguese man-of-war sailing with the wind. Its blue-tinted float, a foot long and eight inches high, acted as a sail.

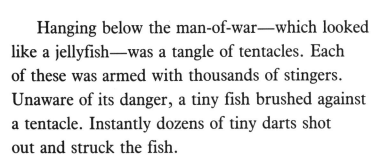

Hanging below the man-of-war—which looked like a jellyfish—was a tangle of tentacles. Each of these was armed with thousands of stingers. Unaware of its danger, a tiny fish brushed against a tentacle. Instantly dozens of tiny darts shot out and struck the fish.

Each dart was attached by a hollow thread to a bag of poison. The bag squeezed, and poison spurted along the hollow thread into the wound. The poison paralyzed the fish. Slowly the man-of-war reeled in the tiny victim to its mouth under the float.

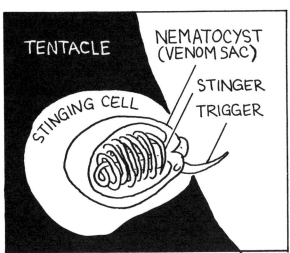

TENTACLE

STINGING CELL

NEMATOCYST (VENOM SAC)

STINGER TRIGGER

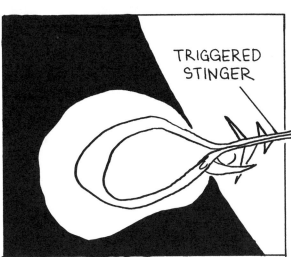

TRIGGERED STINGER

When Voyager bumped against the deadly blue floater, the darts shot out again, but this time they simply fell away. The glass was too hard for the delicate darts to penetrate.

ALONG THE COAST, Voyager met strange companions—plastic bags, Styrofoam cups, a gas can, a bleach bottle, an egg carton, a milk jug, a tangled piece of orange-red fishnet, an electric light bulb. All had been dumped by boats—fishing boats, cargo ships, and passenger liners. The trash littered the sea.

The white towers of Miami Beach shone in the bright sunlight to the west when Voyager was caught in a patch of litter the size of a living room rug.

The entire patch rose and fell in waves rolling toward shore. A thirty-foot sailboat towing a dinghy—a small open boat with oars—appeared and cleaved through the litter. Foot-high white letters on its blue side gave the craft's name: *Sidney's Pride*. No one was on deck, but a man's head and shoulders could be seen through the window of the wheelhouse at the stern, his eyes fixed on the tall buildings onshore.

The sharp bow slicing through the mat of litter set Voyager floating free, along with a plank crusted with barnacles—a kind of shellfish that attaches itself to ship bottoms and floating timbers —and a wooden crate that had once held vegetables.

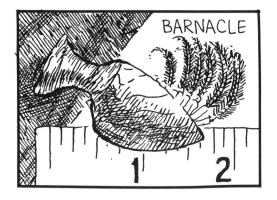

BARNACLE

1   2

In other places along the coast, Voyager passed through the leftovers of an oil spill, some clots as small as a pinhead, others as large as a sandwich. Rubbing against one clot left a black smear on Voyager's side. Some lumps were covered by the tiny shells of sea creatures.

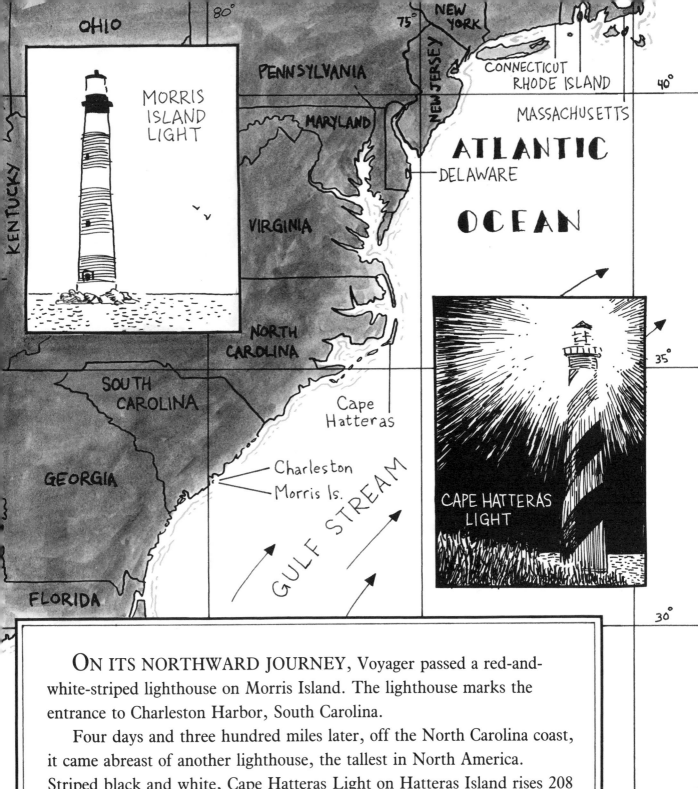

ON ITS NORTHWARD JOURNEY, Voyager passed a red-and-white-striped lighthouse on Morris Island. The lighthouse marks the entrance to Charleston Harbor, South Carolina.

Four days and three hundred miles later, off the North Carolina coast, it came abreast of another lighthouse, the tallest in North America. Striped black and white, Cape Hatteras Light on Hatteras Island rises 208 feet. It was here that Voyager became stranded on a sandy shore.

Earlier that day, Voyager had floated alongside a Wilson's storm-petrel, a chocolate-colored bird with bars of white on its wings and tail. The bird bobbed on the waves. A brown pelican arrived. From thirty feet, it plunged into a school of herring. Two feet below the surface, it scooped a fish into a large pouch below its long bill.

Back on the surface, some three gallons of water drained from the pouch. Then, with an upward toss of its head, the pelican swallowed the fish.

In the afternoon, the water and air turned quiet. On the horizon over the Atlantic, a thundercloud rose into the clear sky. It was four to five miles high and shaped like a cauliflower. It spread sideways, and its top flattened.

First came a flicker of lightning from the dark cloud, followed by a rumble of thunder. The sky above Voyager turned gray, then darker gray. The ocean was hushed. Birds vanished.

At first there was no wind. Then a light breeze sprang up, creating small ripples and smooth, heaving waves. A sudden wind raced across the water, lightning cracked, and thunder boomed. Somewhere in the gray mist, a bell buoy clanged wildly.

Driven toward the beach on mounting waves, Voyager tumbled forward, the tiny stone inside rattling against the glass. Closer and closer it came to shore until one wave, larger than those that had gone before, carried it up the beach and sent it rolling. Along with the bottle came the body of a dead fish sliding up the sand. Both stopped where beach grass began to grow.

Waves advanced on the land, toppling over one another. The wind out of the northeast lashed the sand dunes.

The storm lasted three days. It left Voyager twenty feet from the water, trapped against a foot-high ridge of sand, the message behind the glass barely visible.

Nearby lay a rotting tree stump, a sea traveler from some distant shore deposited here in a final resting place.

That night a raccoon prowling the line of beach grass paused to sniff the cork in the bottle, then ate the dead fish. By morning only the white bones of the skeleton remained.

The storm had left a rich bounty of food for seabirds, crabs, and other beach prowlers. A tangle of seaweed thrown up by the storm waves harbored tiny clams and dead fish. Crabs the size of peas littered the beach along with the bodies of more fish and squid and pieces of wood to which barnacles clung. Sandpipers, plovers, and other shorebirds came to feast, followed by larger herons and egrets.

The storm was also ruthless toward the creations of man.

On the slope of sand above where Voyager lay was an abandoned beach house. It had three redbrick chimneys. The windows had been removed. The house appeared to stare sightless out to sea. Sand had blown into the house through the first-floor windows.

Two men with buckets walked the beach searching for razor clams—slender clams with shells shaped like knife blades. The men stopped, their boots within two feet of the bottle. One man pointed to the empty house.

"I certainly wouldn't build a cottage here," he said. "The dunes shift after every storm and bury anything in their path."

"Dangerous in a storm," the second man said. "No protection from the wind. Waves eat away the shore right up to the front door."

Looking at the house, they missed seeing Voyager and its message.

SUNNY DAYS FOLLOWED. Sand covered all but the neck and cork of the bottle.

Waves heading toward the beach averaged a mere two and a half feet. As each wave receded, sandpipers and plovers pecked at the wet sand. They searched for coquina clams. To feed, the tiny clams extended a tube to draw water from waves washing the beach. The tubes caught and filtered out microscopic bits of food in the water.

A half-dozen clams might live in a handful of sand. Seabirds walking the beach hunted them. To escape an approaching seabird, the clams extended a pink foot and, with swift jerks, dug themselves deeper into the sand away from the pecking bill.

The beach scene was ever-changing. Silver fog settled one morning. A gull drifted out of the fog, banked, and disappeared. A herd of porpoises fed offshore.

On a cloudy afternoon, an elderly woman wearing two sweaters and a rain hat stopped to smell the salt wind and listen for the distant clang of a bell buoy. A man wearing a yellow raincoat and carrying a pail looked for seashells.

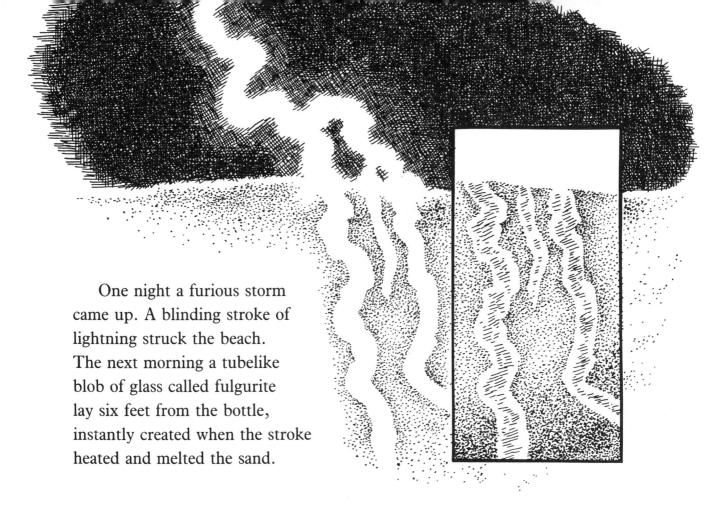

One night a furious storm came up. A blinding stroke of lightning struck the beach. The next morning a tubelike blob of glass called fulgurite lay six feet from the bottle, instantly created when the stroke heated and melted the sand.

MONTHS LATER ANOTHER STORM, fierce and long, started Voyager on its next passage on the ocean sea.

For two days, wind blew away the blanket of dry sand, and the bottle lay exposed, occasionally rocking in its bed, but not moving. Growing waves charged up the beach as if trying to capture the bottle. Then larger waves, formed a week earlier off Africa, began marching in, tirelessly, endlessly, fanning up the beach faster than a man could run, then receding, only to be followed by a fresh wave.

Late on the third morning of the blow, an immense wall of water appeared in the distance and headed for the beach. Trampling over smaller waves, it toppled onto the sand, rushed up the sloping beach, swirled around the bottle, and started it rolling toward the water.

The next wave fell on the bottle, smothering it in foam, and drawing it into the raging sea.

BY LATE SEPTEMBER, Voyager had drifted to Bay Ledge Buoy Number 2. Rising twelve feet out of the water, the buoy marked the entrance to Penobscot Bay, Maine.

A brisk northwest wind blew out of Canada. Taking advantage of tail winds, some twelve million birds a night—shorebirds, such as sandpipers and plovers, and songbirds as small as warblers—passed across the moon.

The birds flew southeast over the ocean in front of approaching cold weather. They headed for islands in the Caribbean and to South America. To reach the islands required sixty-four hours of nonstop flying; South America, about eighty-six hours.

But not all the tiny travelers completed the flight. Some ran into storms—the lucky ones found a ship passing below on which to make a temporary landing. Others were blown far out over the Atlantic. Then, their strength exhausted, they fluttered into the sea and perished. During the birds' autumn flight south, fishermen often found feathers in the stomachs of Atlantic fish.

ATLANTIC OCEAN

Floating north along the Maine coast, Voyager came to a sheltered cove. Above the cove stood a house made of stone with a wide porch and a round tower. A flag flew from the tower.

A girl sat on the railing of the porch, gazing out to sea through a brass telescope.

"What are you looking for?" her father asked.

"Spain is out there," she said.

"Well, it's a bit farther than you can see with my old telescope," he said.

Waves lapped at the rocks and drained through the pebbles on the beach. A fresh breeze came up. The flag on the tower stood stiff. Voyager leaned away from the wind and headed out to sea.

PLANKTON

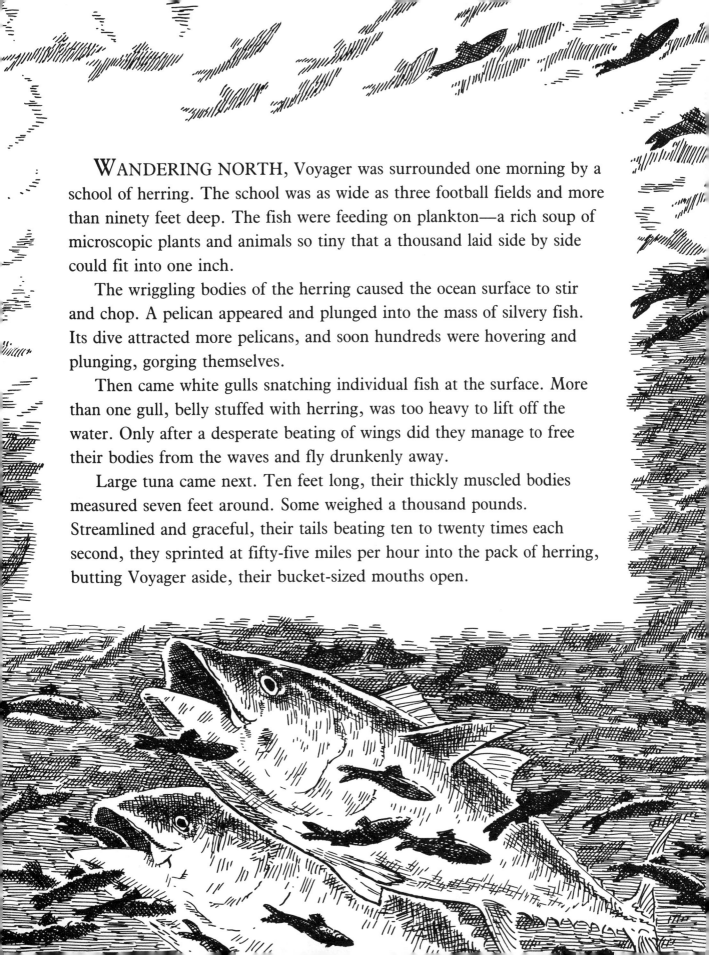

WANDERING NORTH, Voyager was surrounded one morning by a school of herring. The school was as wide as three football fields and more than ninety feet deep. The fish were feeding on plankton—a rich soup of microscopic plants and animals so tiny that a thousand laid side by side could fit into one inch.

The wriggling bodies of the herring caused the ocean surface to stir and chop. A pelican appeared and plunged into the mass of silvery fish. Its dive attracted more pelicans, and soon hundreds were hovering and plunging, gorging themselves.

Then came white gulls snatching individual fish at the surface. More than one gull, belly stuffed with herring, was too heavy to lift off the water. Only after a desperate beating of wings did they manage to free their bodies from the waves and fly drunkenly away.

Large tuna came next. Ten feet long, their thickly muscled bodies measured seven feet around. Some weighed a thousand pounds. Streamlined and graceful, their tails beating ten to twenty times each second, they sprinted at fifty-five miles per hour into the pack of herring, butting Voyager aside, their bucket-sized mouths open.

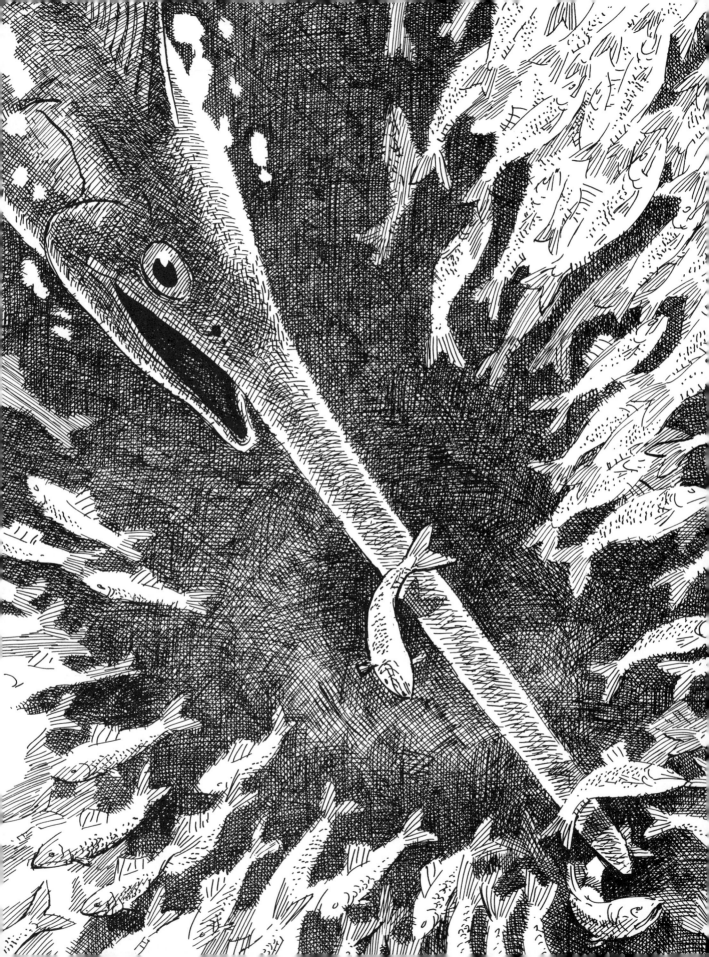

Into this frenzy of fish plunged a swordfish, slashing its four-foot blade violently from side to side, its mouth gaping. The swordfish's tactic was to slash speedily through a school, then return at a more leisurely pace and consume the wounded and dead fish.

A half mile away, a mako shark cruised. Its sensitive hearing detected the herring in distress. One of the fastest fish in the sea, the mako is the only natural enemy of the swordfish.

Now the deadly hunter swung its pointed snout back and forth as it came upon the scent of blood. It followed the scent to the milling herring and, in their midst, the swordfish unhurriedly feeding. Ordinarily, the shark would have fed on the herring, but here was a larger prize.

In the final instant before it was hit, the swordfish leaped fifteen feet high, arching and twisting in a frantic effort to escape its attacker. The mako followed, and the two splashed back among the herring in a cascade of water that engulfed Voyager.

The swordfish might have outswum its pursuer. But this morning its speed would not save it. As it reentered the water, its black eyes spotted two more makos closing in.

Turning to avoid these new enemies, it swung broadside to the first attacker. Instantly two-inch-long teeth sank into its belly and sawed out a twenty-pound chunk. The bite left a perfectly outlined half-moon in the soft belly. The swordfish plunged its blade into the mouth of another attacker, but it broke. The gang of sharks tore at the carcass. The head with the broken sword drifted down into blue darkness.

The birds and the tuna left. The herring continued to feed on the plankton. They survived the attack by the birds and the tuna because of their vast numbers.

Voyager drifted among the silvery fish under a cloudless sky. The water was once again calm.

DAYS LATER, Voyager arrived at the Grand Banks.

East of Newfoundland, the Grand Banks are one of the planet's richest fishing grounds. Along the sand and gravel bottom two hundred feet down, fishermen tow nets to catch cod, haddock, flounder, and pollack.

On this afternoon, Voyager drifted north and east. Streamers of fog trailed above the unruffled water. The air was gray and wet. A seabird flew in and out of the fog. The sun was a pale disk hanging in the sky.

Through a bank of fog came the sounds of men's voices. An engine started, followed by the clank of a winch. The fog parted to reveal a fishing vessel.

On deck, fishermen wore yellow slickers to protect against the damp air. Cables passing over the stern hauled in a net of thrashing fish. Gulls emerged out of the fog as the net was hauled in.

A boy and a man stood at the rail.

The boy was holding a clipboard. He was adding up figures. He said to the captain of the fishing boat, "We have five thousand pounds of haddock, thirty-seven thousand pounds of cod, five hundred of yellowtail, twenty-five hundred lemon sole, forty-five hundred pollack. Looks like a good catch."

The captain frowned. "It's not what you catch, it's what you sell at market. That's what counts."

A gray-green wave lifted Voyager. The bottle slid along the side of the trawler and drifted away into the fog.

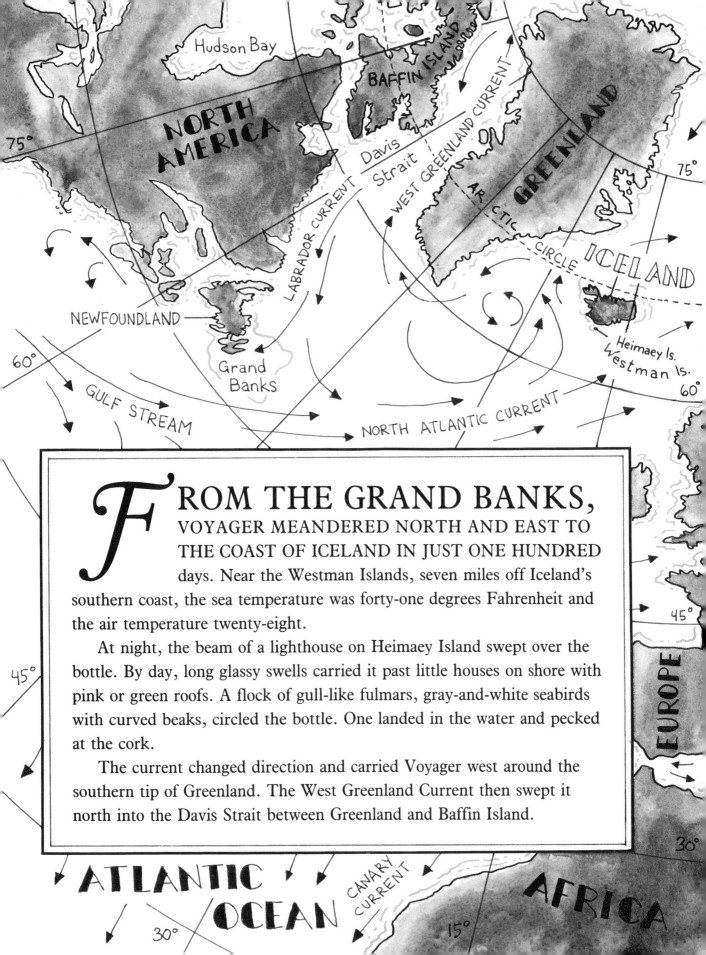

F**ROM THE GRAND BANKS,** VOYAGER MEANDERED NORTH AND EAST TO THE COAST OF ICELAND IN JUST ONE HUNDRED days. Near the Westman Islands, seven miles off Iceland's southern coast, the sea temperature was forty-one degrees Fahrenheit and the air temperature twenty-eight.

At night, the beam of a lighthouse on Heimaey Island swept over the bottle. By day, long glassy swells carried it past little houses on shore with pink or green roofs. A flock of gull-like fulmars, gray-and-white seabirds with curved beaks, circled the bottle. One landed in the water and pecked at the cork.

The current changed direction and carried Voyager west around the southern tip of Greenland. The West Greenland Current then swept it north into the Davis Strait between Greenland and Baffin Island.

Above the Arctic Circle, the bottle strayed among ice pans floating in the quiet water. A narwhal surfaced and glided among the broken pans. A relative of the whale, it was twelve feet long. From its upper jaw protruded an ivory tusk eight feet long. Breathing through its blowhole, the sea creature carefully placed its tapered tusk on an ice pan while resting in the water.

The ice cap on Greenland crept steadily toward the coast and sea, in some places eighty feet in a single day. Chunks the size of apartment buildings broke off and dropped into the water, sending out waves that rocked the ice pans.

A large iceberg measuring fifteen hundred feet long and four hundred feet wide floated out of the water, as tall as a twenty-five-story office building. Some bergs grounded in water five hundred feet deep off Baffin Island. Sharp ridges on their bottoms plowed trenches in the soft sea bottom.

Into "Iceberg Alley" Voyager wandered. The bergs acted like giant refrigerators chilling the air. Water ran in streams down their ice-shiny sides.

At night, a thin film of ice covered the water and held Voyager fast. Under the starry night sky, the giant bergs creaked and groaned as they rocked back and forth in slow motion.

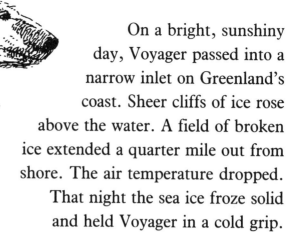

On a bright, sunshiny day, Voyager passed into a narrow inlet on Greenland's coast. Sheer cliffs of ice rose above the water. A field of broken ice extended a quarter mile out from shore. The air temperature dropped. That night the sea ice froze solid and held Voyager in a cold grip.

Day by day the ice field enlarged, spreading into the blue water of the inlet. By the time the polar bear arrived after the seventh day, twenty feet of ice six inches thick held Voyager and separated it from open water.

The thousand-pound, ten-foot-long bear stalked its favorite prey, a seal, now sleeping near an air hole. The bear lay flat. Its long claws, curved and sharp like meat hooks, gripped the ice. Slowly it inched forward.

The seal slept in brief snatches, one minute at a time. Then its eyes opened, scanned the ice for any sign of danger, and closed again.

The bear timed its forward progress for that minute when the seal's eyes were closed. In one hour, it had advanced a cautious ten feet. Before the unsuspecting seal opened its eyes, the bear froze and covered its black eyes and nose with a white paw, still as a hump of snow.

Then the scene changed. The light air shifted and carried the bear's scent to the sleeping seal. Only seconds into its minute of sleep, the seal shot open its eyes and spotted the bear. Frantically it slid on its belly toward the air hole. The bear lunged. It beat the seal to the hole. One blow of its great paw shattered the seal's skull.

Hours later, an arctic fox trotted out on the ice and dined on scraps of meat and fat left behind by the bear.

ONLY A FEW BONES from the luckless seal lay on the ice a few days later when the snarl of an outboard motor echoed between the ice walls bordering the inlet.

Two Eskimo hunters in a skiff carved the dark water. Waves from the boat's passing slapped against the ice sheet in which Voyager was now firmly frozen.

The hunters were two boys barely in their teens. They came from a small village near Cape York.

They had high cheekbones; black hair hung to their shoulders. They wore sealskin jackets and boots of caribou hide. So far, their hunt had not been successful. The outboard motor stopped. The boat drifted. One boy raised his rifle and aimed it at a lone duck on the edge of the ice field.

The bang of the shot sounded like the boom of a cannon as the report bounced against the towering ice walls and rumbled along the inlet. In the distance, a flock of birds feeding on the water took to the air.

Along the edge of the ice cliff above Voyager, a crack appeared as long as a city block. A sound like canvas ripping split the still air as an ice chunk parted from the cliff and slid down toward the water. In midair a chip the size of a school bus separated and crashed through the ice near Voyager. An enormous wave sped outward, shattering the ice field into cakes no larger than cookie pans.

The wave carried the bottle to the center of the inlet, where a current flowed south. Through the loose pack ice it bobbed toward open water.

The frightened young hunters gripped the sides of their rocking boat.

In a hushed voice, one said, "Remember what Father said? 'Do not shoot a gun near the tall ice.' Now I understand his words."

ON THE EDGE of the North Atlantic Current, Voyager traveled east at a speedy one mile per hour.

The ocean's face was constantly changing. When the sky was sunny and blue, the water was brilliant blue. When gray clouds passed in front of the sun, the water took on a gray and gloomy cast.

At dawn, Voyager floated under a bowl of sky that was divided nearly in half, one black and starlit, the second graying with the flush of approaching light. Banks of orange clouds settled on the eastern horizon.

At 4:30 A.M., the sun appeared, and the sky turned pale blue. Red-gold rays burnished the bottle. Another day in its journey began.

Sometimes a week went by with only empty water and sky around the bottle—the sea seemed barren of life. In a dead calm, the ocean was smooth and shiny, round as a sheet of blue glass. No sound. No birds. No ripples. Days passed. Voyager floated alone with the sea and the sun.

Then, suddenly, the sea was no longer empty. A lone gull glided by. Dorado visited—yard-long blue bodies and bright yellow tails—cruising back and forth, the sun striking their flanks. A school of finger-long fish parted as Voyager appeared, then regrouped on the other side. More gulls arrived, crying and mewing, waiting for the tiny fish to rise closer to the surface.

A dolphin swam up, blowing air. For a long minute, it circled the bottle. Once it brought its eye directly up to the glass as if trying to read the message inside.

Dark shearwaters approached on long, curving wings. Gannets—birds with narrow, black-tipped wings spanning five feet—skimmed the water, swerving and climbing to avoid each wave crest.

Once a raft of some twenty-five birds floating on the water broke up and scattered as Voyager drifted toward the edge of the group.

Herring gulls splashed down, scooping up small fish attracted to the bottle, then soared overhead with little movement of their wings.

Small petrels snoozed on the swells, lifting on one wave, descending into the trough, floating light as corks.

Ships appeared from over the horizon, heading west toward New York or Boston or east to Liverpool or London. Some passed close to Voyager, their diesel engines clattering noisily. One went by blaring loud music from a radio.

Trawlers, freighters, and passenger liners cruised by, and then the ocean was quiet again.

Rain showers came every few days. Moisture drawn up from the sea created dark storm clouds. Thunder rumbled and raindrops dimpled the sea, flattening the low waves. The rain sometimes lasted three days. Then it stopped, a rainbow appeared, and Voyager proceeded on a parade of long rollers under a hot sun.

NIGHT ON THE OCEAN. Voyager drifted on a calm sea. Glints of
light, like diamonds in the water, reflected the stars. Shooting stars soared
briefly, then winked out, sparks against the black velvet sky.

Creatures that spent the day in deep water rose to the surface.

First came billions of shrimplike shellfish to feed on tiny plankton.
Deep-sea fish followed, the size and shape of dinner plates. Baby squid
shot six feet out of the water and fell back with light splashes. Sharks
and porpoises arrived to feed on this banquet, nosed the bottle to
determine if it was eatable, then turned away. Something—a
giant squid, perhaps—with cold, unblinking eyes, drifted
up through the water, snaked out long arms, then
sank again into the dark depths.

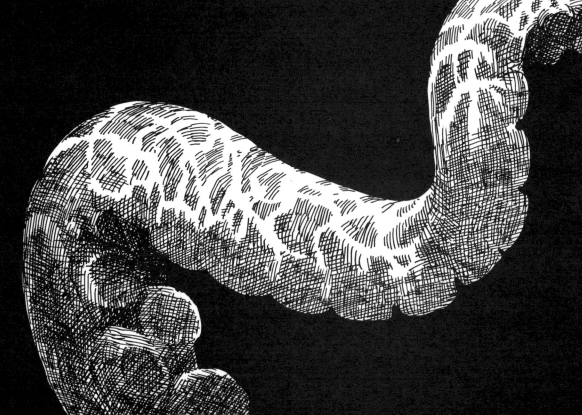

Voyager ghosted along amid this activity,
trailing a shimmering carpet of phosphorescence—
glittering green and yellow flares, like fireflies, on the dark
skin of the sea, a ghostly light given off by tiny plants and animals
drifting near the surface. A wash of water up the neck of the bottle left
a glowing blob of yellow-green fire that then slid away. A large jellyfish,
its float looking like a Chinese lantern, glowed in the dark.
Out of the night the music of a dance band carried across the dark
water. A big passenger liner passed a half mile to the north. Decks and
portholes gleamed with yellow light.

After it passed, the sea was quiet again. The stars blinked. The sea
creatures fed. Voyager's luminous path through the black water vanished
as swiftly as it formed.

THE VOICE WAS HEARD on every ship's radio in the western approaches, the sea-lanes leading to the British Isles.

"This is the British Broadcasting Corporation. Listen now for the morning shipping forecast. Important to ships in the western approaches—southwest strong gale, force nine, increasing to storm, force ten. . . ."

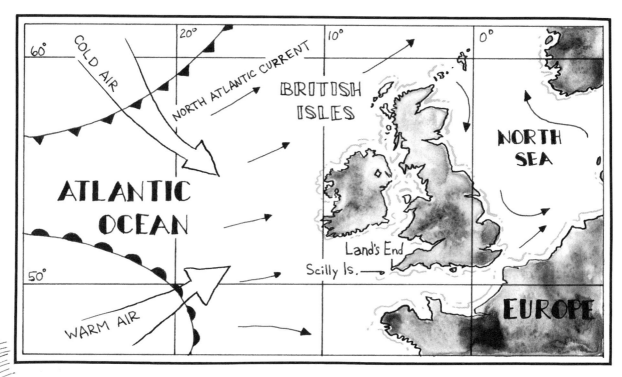

The warning meant:

A low-pressure system—a body of warm air—from the Caribbean Sea and western Atlantic Ocean north of the equator had crossed the Atlantic and was about to enter the area west of the British Isles. Here it would meet—collide, really—with a cold air mass moving southeast from Greenland.

The Central Forecast Office at Bracknell had detected the two movements of air. Forecasters were predicting a severe storm. They had passed the information on to the BBC. A newscaster had then broadcast the warning on the morning weather forecast.

Force nine means gale winds of fifty miles per hour and seas higher than twenty feet. Force ten means winds of seventy-five miles per hour and still-higher waves. Force twelve is the highest rating. It means the severest weather possible and the likelihood of giant waves one hundred feet from bottom to crest.

As the weather warning was broadcast to ships, Voyager floated on a quiet, sun-struck sea. Only a few clouds massed high in the eastern sky. The first indication of the storm was a bare whiff of breeze out of the southwest. Voyager began wending toward the northeast.

Then clouds crept over the western horizon and gradually turned black. The water around Voyager changed from clear blue to gray. In the next three hours, dark clouds tumbled overhead and the wind freshened.

Waves built for the entire day. Voyager surfed down their long sides into boiling troughs of angry water. A heaving wave lifted it skyward, where the wind, now a solid mass, flung it tumbling. The tiny stone inside rattled against its glass prison. Sometimes a foam-topped wave fell *carumpf* on Voyager, burying it in tons of tossing, frothing water.

The wind moaned and tore the tops off the seas. The air was gray with blowing mist. Voyager shot up the slope of a wave, paused, then tobogganed down the far side. Caught in a trough of two rearing waves, it tumbled like a Ping-Pong ball in a washing machine. At other moments it spun gracefully like a ballet dancer. Then another wave caught it and flung it end over end onto the flank of an approaching wave.

The following morning, the radio voice for the BBC stated:

"Winds gusting to seventy-five miles per hour have been recorded. The entire force of the Atlantic sea appears to beat on the southwestern coast of Ireland. Rocks of many tons' weight have been lifted from their beds. Breakers rise to the height of sixty feet. The low-pressure system has deepened alarmingly in the last twelve hours and is entering the area off Land's End."

The radio voice paused, then added, "Worse weather is yet to come."

To build in size and power, the largest waves need six hundred to eight hundred miles of open water. Waves travel in trains of different heights and speed. Two wave trains going in the same direction sometimes get in step and produce a wave that is higher than waves in either train.

But now the unbelievable happened. Three wave trains met. They came together and built into one superwave a hundred feet high. Its life would last but a minute or two before it collapsed, but now its green-black mass was as high as an eight- or nine-story building and as long as a freight train, and seemed to fill the sky. Voyager on its crest was carried along at fifty miles per hour.

In the superwave's path was an ocean liner. The giant wave struck the ship broadside. The liner began to tip, leaning under the brute force of the giant wave.

Voyager swept past the windows of the bridge, where the captain and officers looked helplessly out at the flood of water pouring over the foredeck.

Farther and farther the great liner tipped. Now the rails on the first deck skimmed the sea. A few more feet and it would capsize, fill with water, and sink.

Then the mighty wave passed into the gray darkness. The weight of the heavy engines deep inside the hull began to swing the liner back. Violently the huge vessel rocked back and forth.

Later, the captain said of his ship, "I did not know if she would right herself. In forty years at sea, I've never seen a wave like that. A killer wave!"

For another day, Voyager frisked along, jinking, jouncing, sliding, scooting, tumbling on waves, all pushed by the wind and heading toward the English coast.

On the southwestern edge of the Scilly Isles stands Bishop Rock Light. The 167-foot-high stone lighthouse was sweeping a beam of light across the dark and heaving sea—six flashes of white light, each flash less than one second. It warned ships that they were approaching rocks near the southwestern corner of England.

The powerful beam caught Voyager each time it lifted on a wave. The current carried the bottle traveler past the lighthouse. Its new heading was south and east. The fierce storm was over.

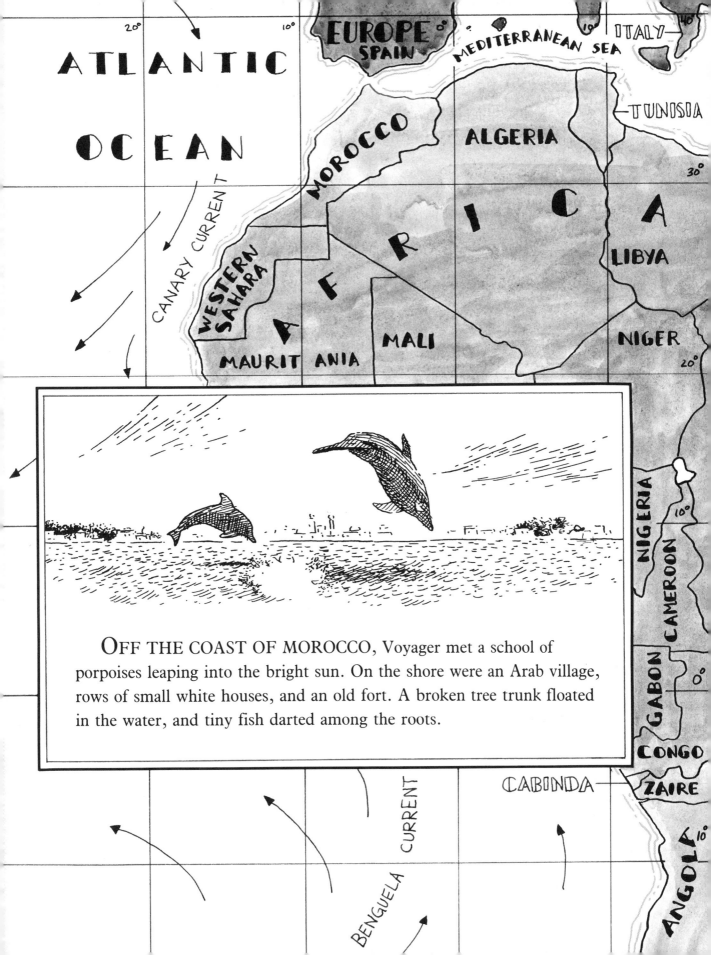

ATLANTIC

OCEAN

EUROPE
SPAIN

MEDITERRANEAN SEA

ITALY

TUNISIA

MOROCCO

ALGERIA

A
F
R
I
C
A

LIBYA

CANARY CURRENT

WESTERN SAHARA

A
F
R
I
C
A

NIGER

MAURITANIA

MALI

NIGERIA

CAMEROON

GABON

CONGO

ZAIRE

CABINDA

BENGUELA CURRENT

ANGOLA

OFF THE COAST OF MOROCCO, Voyager met a school of
porpoises leaping into the bright sun. On the shore were an Arab village,
rows of small white houses, and an old fort. A broken tree trunk floated
in the water, and tiny fish darted among the roots.

90°

45°

NORTH

45°

AMERICA

LABRADOR CURRENT

45°

0°

EUROPE

NORTH ATLANTIC CURRENT

GULF STREAM

BERMUDA

SARGASSO SEA

AZORES

ATLANTIC

CANARY CURRENT

NORTH EQUATORIAL CURRENT

OCEAN

AFRICA

CARIBBEAN CURRENT

0°

PACIFIC OCEAN

45°

THE SARGASSO SEA is a body of water in the mid-Atlantic. It is two thousand miles east to west, and one thousand miles north to south, an area about two-thirds the size of the United States. The Azores Islands lie to the east and the Bahamas to the west.

The Sargasso takes its name from patches of seaweed that spread from horizon to horizon. Storms tear the weed from rocks along the coasts of islands in the Caribbean Sea and Florida. The Gulf Stream flowing north and then east gathers the patches of weed into a great circulating wheel. Little wind or rain enters the region. The water, deep blue, has a high temperature of eighty-three degrees Fahrenheit and is extremely clear.

SARGASSUM FISH

WEST WIND DRIFT

Voyager drifted on the edge of
this dead sea amid patches of weed
the size of doormats. Among the
weeds hid six-inch-long pipefish,
small crabs, and the young of marlin,
swordfish, sailfish, and tuna. Lift
a patch from the water, shake it,
and from the weeds drop tiny sea
slugs, crabs, shrimp, barnacles,
and fish about the size of an
eraser on a pencil.

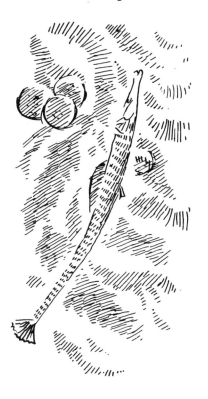

Mats that become loaded with these tiny
creatures grow heavy and begin
to sink. Those creatures able
to swim quickly leave and find another
mat to call home. Those that can't swim,
however, ride a mat to the floor of the ocean
fifteen thousand feet down.
On a favorable current, Voyager skirted the
edge of the Sargasso Sea. Once in the grasp of
the great wheel of sea vegetation, it might have
circled for a thousand years.

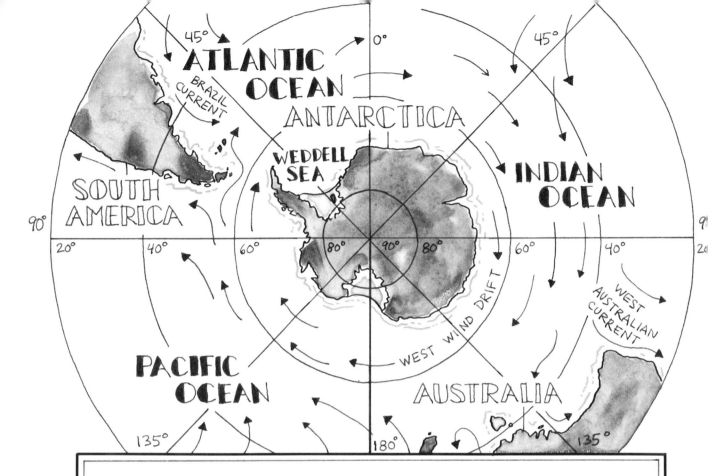

MONTHS AFTER PASSING

MONTHS AFTER PASSING THE SARGASSO SEA, VOYAGER CROSSED AN INVISIBLE LINE IN THE OCEAN. ON ONE side lay the warm waters of the tropics and on the other the cold water of Antarctica.

The ice-capped continent at the earth's "bottom" is about as large as the United States and half of Canada. From the interior, ice flows down to the sea. Reaching the coast, it pushes out in a shelf over deep water. Then, as the tide rises and falls each day, unbearable strains crack the sheet. Pieces float loose.

Some of these pieces are fifty miles long and a thousand feet thick. The icebergs are flat—unlike Greenland's, which are mountainous. These giant bergs, some larger than the state of Rhode Island, travel north toward the tropics. From a distance, the bergs look like white marble cliffs floating in the sea.

Voyager entered the Weddell Sea in early January, the ice continent's midsummer. The sea around the ice holds one of the richest colonies of life on the planet.

Supporting this vast community are krill. Shrimplike creatures about two inches long, they are the main food of fish, seals, penguins, seabirds, and whales. Each year, the Antarctic spawns a billion and a half tons of krill. The krill travel in schools so vast that satellites hundreds of miles up in space can detect them.

Where Voyager drifted, blue whales cruised nearby. Into their open mouths volumes of water poured. The water strained through baleen strainers— bonelike plates—hanging down each side of their jaws like curtains. Krill were caught in the baleen. Now and then a whale's large tongue wiped the baleen clean and passed the food into its gullet.

KRILL

1　2

The blue's cousin, the humpback whale, used another hunting technique. To trap a feast of krill, a humpback swam in circles underwater. As it swam, it exhaled air bubbles. The rising bubbles created a kind of fence enclosing the krill. Then the whale—some forty-nine feet long and weighing thirty-five tons—swam up the column of krill with mouth open.

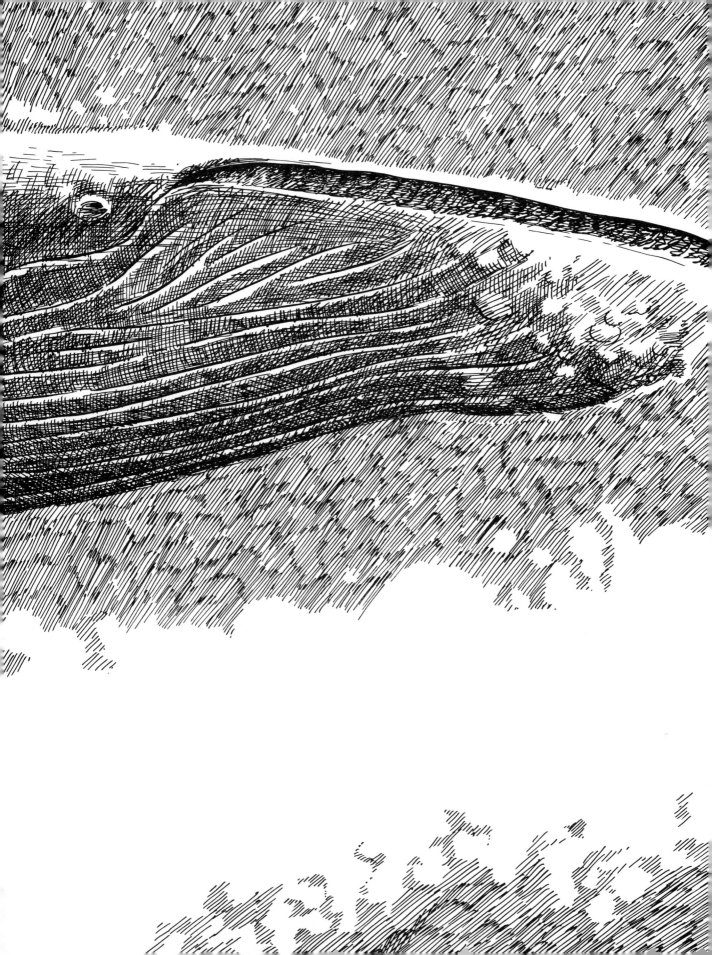

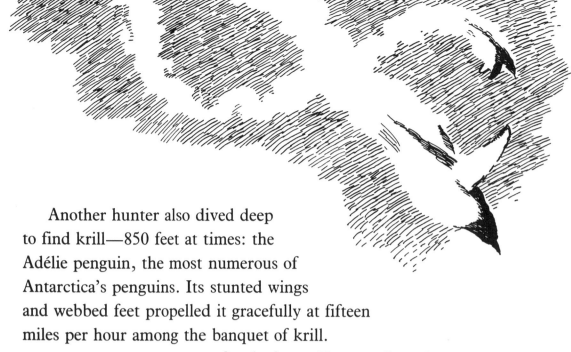

Another hunter also dived deep to find krill—850 feet at times: the Adélie penguin, the most numerous of Antarctica's penguins. Its stunted wings and webbed feet propelled it gracefully at fifteen miles per hour among the banquet of krill.

On the ice as Voyager floated closer, a hundred thousand Adélies tended their chicks. The parent birds built circular nests of pebbles and bits of bone. One mate returned from the sea, its crop—a baglike pouch in its throat—filled with krill for the pair of downy chicks. Then the partner tobogganed across the ice on its belly to join its fellows at the edge of the ice shelf.

But at the edge there was hesitation. Not one wanted to jump seven feet into the twenty-eight-degree water. As more crowded the edge, however, one brave penguin, pressed from behind, sprang from the edge, and the others followed. Voyager bobbed on the waves created by hundreds of penguins leaping into the sea at the same time.

On this morning, though, unknown to the Adélies, a leopard seal hid under an overhanging ledge of ice. When the first Adélie leaped, the hunter waited. When a hundred had splashed into the water, it dived.

The leopard seal was ten feet long. Its deep jaw held sharp, inward-slanting teeth. The appearance of the hunter in their midst underwater caused the Adélies to panic. Speeding to the surface, they vaulted seven feet straight up onto the ice shelf.

The leopard seal surfaced with an Adélie clamped by the head. Furiously it whipped the luckless bird back and forth until the penguin's gashed skin peeled back and turned inside out. Feasting on the warm flesh, the leopard seal left a clean skeleton. Gulls flocked down to snatch scraps of floating flesh.

But the leopard seal's capture of the penguin did not go unseen. A quarter mile away, six killer whales cruised. Their six-foot-high fins sliced the water. The killers feed on fish, seals, penguins, walruses, squid, porpoises, and sperm whales. Fast and strong, they have no natural enemies. Their backs are midnight black and their bellies and throats vivid white.

The leader—twenty-five feet long, weighing six tons—lifted out of the water to scan the sea for prey. Its small eye spotted the leopard seal and the Adélies leaping from the water to the ice shelf. The bull led his five fellows toward the scene.

The leopard seal saw the fins of the approaching killer whales. It had survived for years in this harsh ice world because it was always alert. Frantically it scrambled onto an ice pan. In the center it would be safe.

The killer whales circled, their small eyes focused on the nervous leopard seal. As though on signal, the killers placed their massive heads on the pan and tried to tip it and send the leopard seal sliding into their jaws. But the pan was too broad to tip.

The killers then dived under the ice sheet and tried to lift it. They battered the pan from below. The frightened leopard seal dug its claws into the ice. The ice was too thick to break.

Now the killer whales backed off. They huddled together as if holding a conference. Then all turned and in line rushed the ice pan at their full twenty-five-mile-per-hour speed. Their massive heads pushed a wave of water.

At the instant before crashing into the pan, they dived. The wave of water continued. It washed across the ice sheet and swept the startled leopard seal off the far edge. The killers, having swum under the pan, were waiting.

In time, the water quieted. Watched by the Adélies, the killer whales passed around the edge of the ice shelf and headed out to sea. The wave created by their powerful bodies passing through the water caused Voyager to spin in place. One young killer eyed the bottle, but ignored it in favor of keeping up with the group.

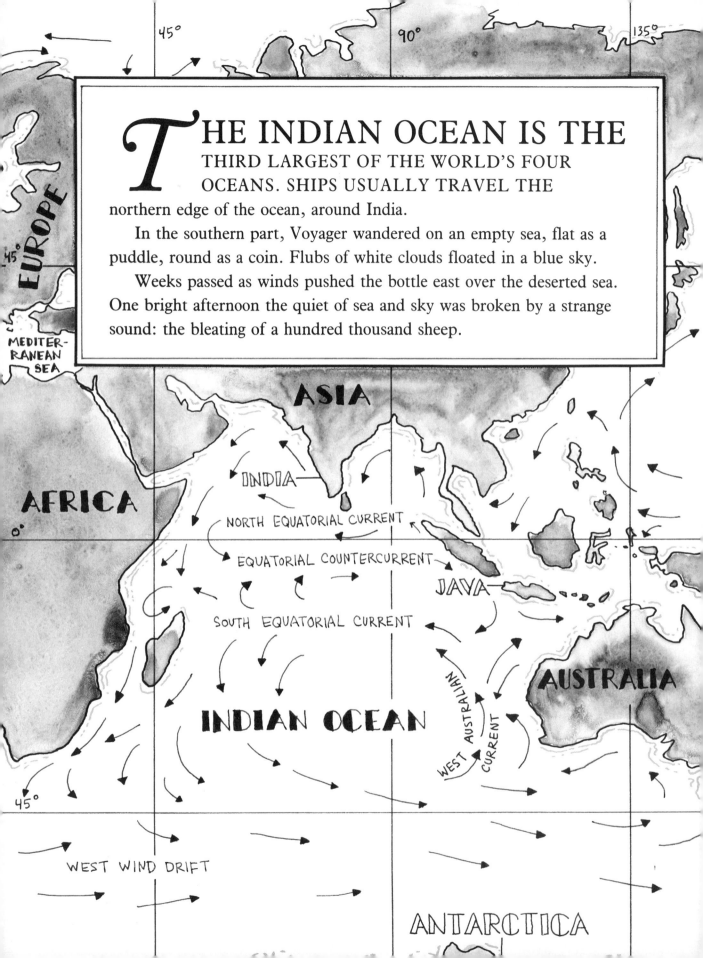

45°   90°   135°

EUROPE

45°

MEDITER-
RANEAN
SEA

THE INDIAN OCEAN IS THE THIRD LARGEST OF THE WORLD'S FOUR OCEANS. SHIPS USUALLY TRAVEL THE

northern edge of the ocean, around India.

In the southern part, Voyager wandered on an empty sea, flat as a puddle, round as a coin. Flubs of white clouds floated in a blue sky.

Weeks passed as winds pushed the bottle east over the deserted sea. One bright afternoon the quiet of sea and sky was broken by a strange sound: the bleating of a hundred thousand sheep.

ASIA

AFRICA

INDIA

0°

NORTH EQUATORIAL CURRENT

EQUATORIAL COUNTERCURRENT

JAVA

SOUTH EQUATORIAL CURRENT

INDIAN OCEAN

AUSTRALIA

WEST AUSTRALIAN CURRENT

45°

WEST WIND DRIFT

ANTARCTICA

A quarter mile north, on a course from Fremantle, Australia, passed the *Nelly G.*, a sheep ship. Behind the bridge were stacked open pens seven decks high. The pens held 115,000 sheep. The animals were headed for ports in the desert kingdoms east of the Mediterranean Sea.

As the floating stockyard headed for the horizon, the sea became quiet again.

VOYAGER ROAMED TOWARD JAVA, a large island northwest of Australia, and there it met one of the world's deadliest snakes.

A party of the yellow serpents rose from their hunting grounds three hundred feet down. A long lung from its throat almost to its tail enabled each snake to stay underwater for hours without breathing.

Now the snakes sunned in the warm water near the surface. Nostrils on top of their snouts enabled them to float near the surface to take in fresh air. Their skin was waterproof. The sky was empty of birds. Sharks were their only other enemy. Even though its fangs were small and its bite hardly deep enough to draw blood, the sea snake had poison more powerful than a king cobra's. The yellow snakes swam for Voyager, their flat tails paddling from side to side like oar blades. Their forked tongues flicked in and out to get a sense of the bottle. Then, when Voyager made no threatening move, they came even closer until their tongues "tasted" the smooth glass. One bit into the cork, injecting a droplet of venom strong enough to stop the heart of a two-hundred-pound man. With the cork, though, the only result was a broken fang. After minutes of curious inspection, the snakes swam off. White seabirds appeared in the sky and the group dived. One bird descended on Voyager, fluttering its wings as it hovered for a close inspection, then glided away over the polished surface of the sea.

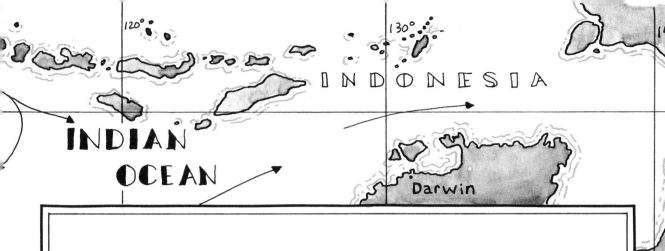

VOYAGER CAME TO REST in a freshwater swamp at the mouth of a broad stream in Kakadu National Park on Australia's northern coast, east of Darwin. The incoming tide flowing into the swampy stream had lodged the bottle in a patch of reeds. Nearby, a saltwater crocodile lay motionless as a log.

The crocodile was nearly seventeen feet long and weighed seventeen hundred pounds. Thick neck muscles supported a heavy head equipped with seventy teeth. Only its yellow eyes and nostrils protruded from the water.

The "saltie"—as residents of the coast called the dangerous animals—could run on land at ten to fifteen miles per hour and swim twenty miles per hour in water. Its powerful tail could propel a saltie straight up and almost out of the water to snatch a flying bird.

This saltie waited at a place where kangaroos, horses, and buffalo came to the stream to drink. It could eat an entire horse in just two days.

A large buffalo came to the water's edge and lowered its head to drink. The crocodile sank below the water. Stubby legs pulled it swiftly over the bottom mud toward the animal. The saltie could see the buffalo's nose in the water, its tongue creating ripples as it drank.

Lunging from the bottom, the crocodile seized the buffalo
by the snout and pulled the animal into the water. Using its
powerful tail as a lever, it toppled the buffalo over on its side.
The unfortunate beast was then tugged
into deep water and drowned.
As the thrashing water quieted,
the bottle, freed from
the patch of reeds,
drifted into the stream.

THERE WERE TWO IN THE BOAT, and a dog.

The father pulled at the oars. His daughter sat in the stern next to a black-and-white terrier. The dog placed its paws on the board seat and barked at something in the water.

The father was a handsome man with gray curly hair and skin the color of cocoa. He said, "The mutt thinks he is tough. Old Sal-tie could swallow him like a witchetty grub." He spoke slowly and distinctly.

The girl watched the crocodile following the boat, yellow eyes just above the water, eyeing the dog. She held the dog's mouth closed so it wouldn't bark.

"I remember old Sal-tie," the father said. "A powerful beast. He's the one bit the propeller off my motor. No bullets for my rifle, so I clubbed him with the butt—on the snout. He did not like that and swam away." He chuckled. "Throw him the dog, Coleen. (*Throw heem the dawg, Kawleen.*) Then old Sal-tie will let us alone."

The dog, watching the crocodile coming closer, shrank into the girl's arms.

"The mutt will take care of his hunger—for a time," the father said. "He is only a stray you found."

The girl clutched the shivering dog. Her eyes pleaded. "Please . . . I want to keep him."

The father rowed faster. "Come now, Coleen. I recognize your feeling for the an-i-mal. It can be either his life or ours."

Holding the dog, the girl slid off the seat and huddled on the bottom of the boat. "Now he can't see us. See if he'll leave."

It was true. With the dog out of sight, the crocodile dropped behind. It sank beneath the muddy surface.

"My gosh, will you look at that!" the father exclaimed. "Old Sal-tie! Plenty tough, but not too bright. A brain the size of my little finger. He can't see you, so he thinks you have gone. That was clever."

He marveled at his daughter . . . so bright. Now she wanted to become an astronomer . . . study the stars. Amazing.

The girl sat on the rear seat. She looked over the stream and pointed. "There's a bottle floating in the water—over there. Something's inside."

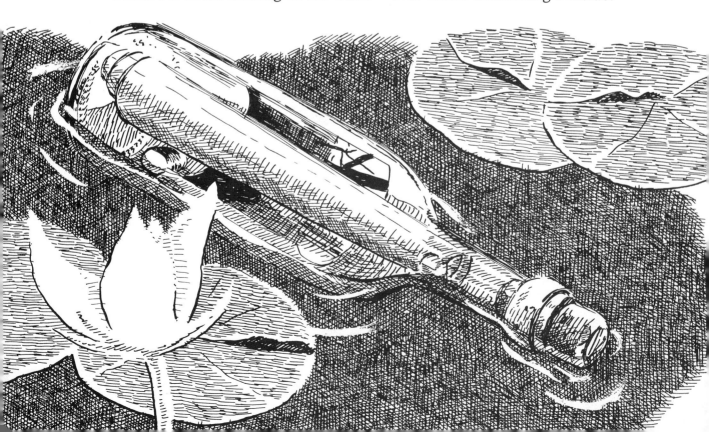

COLEEN SHOWED THE BOTTLE to her mother, who was sitting on the sofa knitting a sweater. The black-and-white dog lay next to a basket holding balls of yarn. Its head rested on one of the mother's slippers.

"Look, Mum. There's a message inside."

The mother put down the sweater and knitting needles. "A message! Well, look at that! Maybe it will tell where to find buried treasure."

"Oh, Mum, be serious," the girl scolded gently. She twisted the cork. "It's crumbly . . . maybe it won't come out. There! I've got it." She shook the bottle. "There's a stone inside. Listen!" She shook the bottle, and the stone rattled against the glass.

Her father came into the living room with a hammer. "Give me the bottle and I will break it. Else how will we get the message out."

The dog raised its head to watch.

"Do we have to break it?" Coleen cried, alarmed. "Maybe it traveled a long way to get here. . . ."

"My father and grandfather were fishermen," the mother said. "I remember them saying, 'The sea wipes away all footprints.' The only way to know where the bottle came from is to read the message." She picked up her knitting. The needles clicked. "Give it to your father."

The father reached for the bottle. "I will take it outside and break it."

The girl drew away, holding the bottle tight to her chest. "No, oh no!" Then her eyes caught the glint of her mother's knitting needles. "Wait! Maybe I can remove the message without breaking the bottle."

"Coleen . . ." The mother frowned, a displeased note in her voice. The girl took two knitting needles from the basket of yarn at her mother's feet. Carefully she inserted one needle through the neck of the bottle so it went between the message and the glass. The second needle went on the inside of the message. Then she turned the needles until the message curled tightly around them. Slowly she drew the needles and message through the neck of the bottle. "Got it!"

The father smiled fondly. "Clever."

The girl turned the bottle upside down. The stone, a polished agate, brown with red and blue bands, dropped into her hand.

Then she unfolded the damp paper. A snapshot dropped out. It showed a boy with rust-colored hair. One eye was nearly closed from squinting in the sun. He wore braces on his teeth.

"Some of the writing is blurry," Coleen said. "Water must have leaked around the cork. . . ."

She read the letter. "The boy
lives in . . . in Minnesota. In America."

"Hold there!" the father said. "Where is
Minnesota in America? It's a big country."

He took an atlas from the bookcase. "Let me see. North
America . . . yes, Minnesota is here—in the center of the country,
on the border of Canada."

The mother gasped. "On the other side of the world!"

"The boy writes: 'In school, I read a book about messages found
in floating bottles. When I went with my family to an island in
the Caribbean Sea, I thought of sending a bottle message.
Who would find it? Where would it end up—on
what distant shore? What adventures would
it have? To the finder—please write and tell me
where you find the bottle. I have named it Voyager.' "

The girl looked up from the letter. "Do
you have the stone, Mum? Here he tells why
he placed it in the bottle. . . ."

" 'To the finder,' " she read. " 'I am sending you a stone, a special charm. It comes from the shore of Lake Superior. In Minnesota, the Cherokee Indians tell an old story about special stones. Take the stone and hold it. It is a Voyager's Stone. If you hold it long enough, it will speak to you. It will tell you there are no enemies in the path before you, that all you meet are friends. The stone talks to you, not in words, but in a language that needs no words.' "

The mother looked at her daughter. "Yes, I have heard about the Voyager's Stone. It is a charm to carry with us on our journey . . . to help us find courage. . . ."

"Yes, I know the story," the father said. "Our people have told it for hundreds of years."

FOR A WEEK the bottle stayed on the mantel over the fireplace in the main room. Coleen wrote to the boy in Minnesota. She told about Old Saltie and where she had found the bottle. Yes, her mother and father also knew the story of the Voyager's Stone. Indeed, when she held the stone, it did speak to her. She would keep it always.

Days later, she looked at Voyager on the mantel. It seemed out of place. She took the bottle to her room and placed it on her chest of drawers. Then she tried it on her bedside table, next to the alarm clock. Still the bottle looked strange. It didn't belong in the room.

The day before school began, she had an idea.

She took Voyager to the kitchen table and there composed a letter. Carefully she rolled the letter and inserted it through the neck of the bottle. In the garden she found a stone, washed and dried it, and dropped it in the bottle: *plink!* She found a new cork.

That evening when the tide was going out in Van Diemen Gulf, Coleen took Voyager down to the water. The black-and-white dog followed her. She talked to the bottle.

"Ahead await new adventures. Maybe someday I'll get a letter from the person who finds you."

For a long moment she gazed over the water. Then, with all her strength, she hurled Voyager as far as she could.

"Be an explorer!" she called.

Voyager splashed into the water and bobbed to the surface.

To the west, the sun had just sunk below the horizon. In the east, above a dark point of land, stars were beginning to show in the night sky.

The outflowing tide carried Voyager away from the land and onto the vast ocean sea.